Solar System

by Lisa E. Greathouse

Science Contributor
Sally Ride Science
Science Consultants
Nancy McKeown, Planetary Geologist
William B. Rice, Engineering Geologist

MISSION: SCIENCE

Developed with contributions from Sally Ride Science™

Sally Ride
Science

Sally Ride Science™ is an innovative content company dedicated to fueling young people's interests in science.

Our publications and programs provide opportunities for students and teachers to explore the captivating world of science—from astrobiology to zoology.

We bring science to life and show young people that science is creative, collaborative, fascinating, and fun.

To learn more, visit www.SallyRideScience.com

First hardcover edition published in 2009 by
Compass Point Books
151 Good Counsel Drive
P.O. Box 669
Mankato, MN 56002-0669

Editor: Mari Bolte
Designer: Heidi Thompson
Editorial Contributor: Sue Vander Hook

Art Director: LuAnn Ascheman-Adams
Creative Director: Joe Ewest
Editorial Director: Nick Healy
Managing Editor: Catherine Neitge

 This book was manufactured with paper containing at least 10 percent post-consumer waste.

Library of Congress Cataloging-in-Publication Data
Greathouse, Lisa E.
  Solar system / by Lisa E. Greathouse.
       p. cm. — (Mission: Science)
  Includes index.
  ISBN 978-0-7565-4071-5 (library binding)

1. Solar system—Juvenile literature. I. Title. II. Series.
  QB501.3.G79 2009
  523.2—dc22   2008035728

Visit Compass Point Books on the Internet at *www.compasspointbooks.com*
or e-mail your request to *custserv@compasspointbooks.com*

Table of Contents

Our Place in the Universe 6

The Sun 8

The Planets... 10

Mercury and Venus 12

Life on Earth 14

Mars and Jupiter 18

Saturn and Uranus... 20

Neptune and Dwarf Planet Pluto........................ 22

Dwarf Planets.. 24

Asteroids, Meteoroids, and Comets..................... 26

Constellations.. 28

      Science Activity..................................... 30

      Important People in Astronomy 33

      Glossary.. 34

      Astronomy Through Time 36

      Additional Resources 38

      Index... 39

      About the Author 40

Our Place in the Universe

Have you ever looked into the night sky and wondered what was out there? Have you seen the twinkling lights and imagined what they looked like up close? Perhaps you've pictured Earth as one of those tiny spots and thought about our place in the universe. People have been gazing into the heavens for thousands of years, hoping to find answers to their questions about outer space. Until the mid-1500s, scientists thought Earth, not the sun, was the center of our solar system.

Ancient scientists believed that everything revolved around Earth. Nicolaus Copernicus, however, had a different idea. He said the sun, not Earth, is the center of our solar system. It was a radical idea at that time, and few believed that Earth and the other planets revolved around the sun. Scientists eventually proved that Copernicus was right. Earth is one of at least eight planets in our solar system that travel around the sun.

Space Wanderers

Ancient Greeks noticed that some celestial bodies change their positions in the sky. They seemed to wander. What the Greeks saw were planets. They called them *planetai*, a word that means "wanderer." Today we know that each planet moves in an invisible path around the sun. That path is called an orbit.

Did You Know?

Light travels at about 186,000 miles (299,000 kilometers) per second. It can travel between Earth and the moon in 1.3 seconds—it would take more than nine years for a human to walk that distance.

The sun, eight planets and their moons, one dwarf planet, and countless meteors, asteroids, and comets make up our solar system.

Astronomers also discovered that our solar system is not the only thing in space. It is located at the edge of the Milky Way galaxy, which has about 200 billion stars. And that's not everything out there. The Milky Way is only one of at least 100 billion galaxies in the universe. Each galaxy is made up of billions of stars.

We know more about the Milky Way than other galaxies because Earth is part of it. Our galaxy is in the shape of a spiral, and thus it is called a spiral galaxy. It can be seen on a very dark night as a bright band in the sky. Its expanse is so huge that light would take 100,000 years to travel across it.

The Sun

The planets orbit the sun, a very large, bright, and extremely hot star. Although it is not the biggest or brightest star in the Milky Way galaxy, it is the largest celestial body in our solar system. In fact, it contains 99.8 percent of all the combined mass of our solar system. It would take about 333,000 planets the size of Earth to equal the mass of the sun.

The sun, at the center of our solar system, is Earth's major source of energy. It gives our planet both light and heat. Without the sun, Earth would be extremely cold, too cold for any living thing to survive. The sun is also responsible for wind, ocean currents, the water cycle, and plant growth.

Like other stars, the sun is made of very hot hydrogen and helium gases. The temperature at the center is about 27 million degrees Fahrenheit (15 million degrees Celsius). Scientists, of course, cannot go into the center of the sun to measure the temperature. Instead, they use mathematical equations that are based on laws of physical science.

Because the sun is so enormous, it has more gravity than the planets. The force of its gravity keeps Earth and the other planets in their places and holds them in their orbits around the sun. The sun's extreme gravity also keeps its own hot gases from escaping into space.

The Sun God

In ancient Greek and Roman mythology, the sun god was Apollo. He rode a chariot across the sky every day to provide heat and light for Earth.

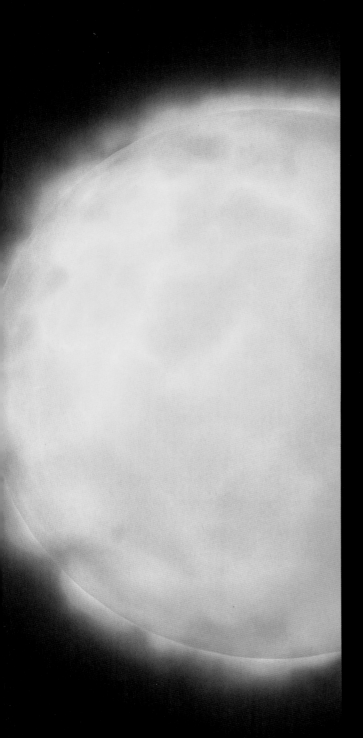

Extreme Gravity—Black Holes

Huge stars that use up all their energy form what are called black holes. As a star dies from lack of energy, its gravity causes it to collapse in on itself. The force of its gravity is now so great that not even light can escape. A black hole is not really a hole. It is an area of space that is very crowded with a lot of matter in a small space. Gravity has smashed the matter together, or compressed what used to be a massive star.

We can't see black holes. We only know a black hole exists because objects in space are forcefully pulled toward that area. Once an object enters a black hole, the object disappears. In 2008, scientists identified the smallest black hole yet discovered in our galaxy. It measures only 15 miles (24 km) in diameter. But it weighs 3.8 times more than the sun.

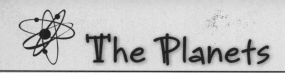

"My Very Educated Mother Just Served Us Nachos." For years, people have used a sentence like this to remember the names of the eight planets. The first letter of each word stands for a planet—M for Mercury, V for Venus, and so on. It also helps us remember the order of the planets from the sun. The closest planet to the sun is Mercury. After that are Venus, Earth, Mars, Jupiter, Saturn, Uranus, and Neptune.

A planet is a large celestial body that revolves around a star in space. It also reflects that star's light. The planets in our solar system revolve around the sun.

Most of the planets also have one or more moons traveling around them. As the planets revolve around the sun, they also spin, or rotate. This is why we have day and night. When part of Earth rotates away from the sun, it is night. On the other side of Earth, it is daytime. The time it takes for a planet to rotate once is the planet's day. It takes Earth 24 hours to make one rotation. This means that Earth's day is 24 hours long.

A planet's year is the number of days it takes for it to orbit the sun. The planets nearest the sun move the fastest. Mercury, the closest planet to the sun, orbits the sun once every 88 Earth days. Neptune, the farthest planet from the sun, takes 60,225 Earth days (or 165 Earth years).

Did You Know?

It takes Earth 365.25 days to travel once around the sun. Every four years, an extra day is added to the month of February to realign Earth's calendar with the sun. These years are called leap years.

What Would You Weigh on Another Planet?

When you stand on a scale on Earth, your weight is measured by the pull of gravity between you and Earth. You could weigh more or less on another planet, depending on its pull of gravity. The strength of that pull depends on how massive (or heavy) the planet is. Mass is different. For example, a small rock has more mass than a large inflated balloon.

On planets with less mass than Earth, you would weigh less. On planets with more mass, you would weigh more. If you weighed 100 pounds (45 kilograms) on Earth, you would weigh only 38 pounds (17 kg) on Mercury. Mercury has much less mass than Earth. If you could stand on Jupiter, you would weigh 236 pounds (107 kg). Jupiter's mass is huge. It would take about 318 Earths to equal the mass of Jupiter.

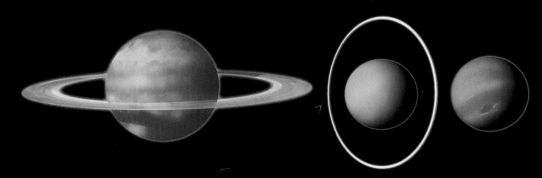

Mercury and Venus

Mercury is the closest planet to the sun. It is the smallest of the four inner planets, which also include Venus, Earth, and Mars.

Mercury is covered with craters, or shallow depressions, caused by space objects that struck its surface. Because Mercury is so close to the sun, it is very hot—hot enough to melt lead. Its highest temperature is 797 F (425 C). But at night, it can get as cold as minus 238 F (minus 150 C). The huge difference in temperature is because Mercury has very long days. Being so near the sun for that long makes the planet very hot. Both days and nights on Mercury are about 59 Earth days each. It can get very cold when the planet does not receive heat from the sun for 59 days.

Venus, the second planet from the sun, is the hottest planet in our solar system. It's also the brightest planet in the night sky. It gets hotter than Mercury because thick clouds surrounding it hold in the sun's heat. It can get as hot as 864 F (462 C).

Did You Know?

Thirteen times each century, viewers on Earth can watch as Mercury passes in front of the sun. This is called a transit. The first two transits of the 21st century occurred in 2003 and 2006. The next transit is not until 2016.

Venus ➡

Venus is slightly smaller than Earth. It spins much more slowly, though. It takes 243 Earth days for Venus to spin once. It takes 225 Earth days for Venus to orbit the sun.

⬅ Mercury

Goddess Planet

All the planets in our solar system except Earth are named after Roman deities. Venus is the only planet named for a goddess. The mythological Venus was the Romans' symbol of love and beauty. Venus is the brightest planet in the solar system and one of the brightest lights in the sky. Everything on the surface of Venus is named after goddesses and other women in history and literature.

13

Earth is unlike any other planet in our solar system. It is the only planet known to have life. It is also the only planet with water in the form of oceans, lakes, and rivers. Venus has rain, but the water has a high level of acid. The planet is also too hot to sustain lakes and oceans. We know that water is necessary for life as we know it on Earth. Water covers three-quarters of Earth's surface, which makes the planet appear blue from outer space. Earth is also unique because its atmosphere contains oxygen, which is necessary for humans and animals to breathe. The atmosphere also protects us from the deadly rays of the sun.

Earth is the third planet from the sun and the fourth smallest. As it orbits the sun, Earth rotates at a speed of 1,031 miles (1,660 km) per hour. In 24 hours, it makes a single rotation, or one Earth day.

"One Small Step for Man"

On July 20, 1969, more than 600 million people got together at restaurants, homes, and moonwalk parties to watch television. It seemed as if the whole world held its breath, wondering whether the first humans would land on the moon. People around the world cheered and clapped as the *Eagle*, the landing portion of the spacecraft *Apollo 11*, landed on the moon. Inside the *Eagle* were American astronauts Neil Armstrong and

Buzz Aldrin. Astronaut Michael Collins orbited above in the spacecraft. A camera in the module provided live television coverage. Then astronaut Neil Armstrong stepped out in his spacesuit, walked down a ladder, and set foot on the moon. History had been made—a human had walked on the surface of Earth's moon for the first time. As viewers watched and listened, Armstrong said: "One small step for man, one giant leap for mankind."

The Four Seasons

The four seasons on Earth (winter, spring, summer, and fall) occur because Earth is tilted on its axis. For part of the year, the northern hemisphere, or top half of Earth, leans toward the sun and gets direct sunlight. During that time, that part of Earth experiences summer with higher temperatures. At the same time, the southern hemisphere is leaning away from the sun, receiving less sunlight. That part of Earth experiences winter.

The seasons' weather conditions depend on where you live on Earth. For example, people who live in the northern hemisphere are used to cold winters and warm summers. But those who

Did You Know?

Moons orbit most of the planets in our solar system. Saturn has the most moons, while Earth has just one. Earth's moon is nearly as big as the planet Mercury.

Solstices and Equinoxes

In the northern hemisphere, solstices occur when the sun reaches the northernmost or southernmost points in the sky, causing the shortest or longest day of the year. Solstices are always on June 20 or 21, the first day of summer, and December 21 or 22, the first day of winter.

Equinoxes occur when Earth's equator is parallel to the sun's rays, causing 12 hours of daylight and 12 hours of darkness. Equinoxes are always on March 21 or 22, the first day of spring, and September 22 or 23, the first day of fall.

Winter

The sunlight in the southern hemisphere is spread out over a larger area, decreasing the sun's intensity

Day Night

Night Day

The Sun

Summer

The northern hemisphere gets concentrated sunlight, making the sun's heat more intense

live on the southern hemisphere spend June inside and December on the beach!

The tilt of Earth never changes. What changes is Earth's position in its orbit around the sun. As Earth goes around the sun, some parts get more sunlight than others, and thus the planet has changing seasons.

Earth's Name

Earth is the only planet in our solar system that is not named after a god. Its name comes from the Old English word *eorthe*, which means "ground." However, the Roman goddess who symbolized Earth was named Terra, which is the word for Earth in several languages, including Latin, Italian, and Portuguese.

Mars and Jupiter

Mars is a cold, windy planet. The largest mountains in the solar system are found on Mars. Its tallest mountain, a volcano, rises more than three times higher than Earth's loftiest peak. Mars is sometimes called the Red Planet because of its reddish-colored soil, which is rich in the mineral iron oxide.

Mars, the fourth planet from the sun, is about half the size of Earth. Its average temperature is about minus 140 F (minus 95 C). Scientists think water may have flowed on Mars millions of years ago. They are still looking for signs that there may have once been life on the planet.

Jupiter, the fifth planet from the sun, is the largest planet in the solar system and more massive than the other seven planets combined. It is one of four giant planets made of gases. Jupiter is encircled by three faint rings and has at least 63 moons. Its main feature is the Great Red Spot, a huge, violent storm larger than Earth itself. This storm has lasted at least 300 years.

Mars ➡

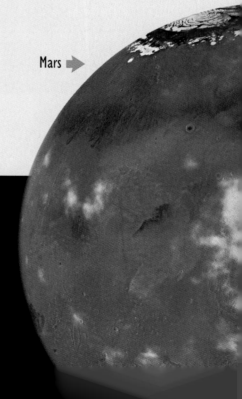

The Gods and the Planets

Ancient astronomers named the planet Mars after a mythological Roman god of war. The planet's red color made people think of the blood of battle. The planet Jupiter was named after the mythological king of all Roman gods and ruler of the universe. It was an appropriate name for the largest of all planets.

◄ Two rovers named *Spirit* and *Opportunity* have explored Mars for more than four years.

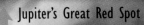

▲ Jupiter's Great Red Spot

Saturn and Uranus

Many people think Saturn is the most beautiful planet because of the thousands of rings that encircle it. These rings are made mostly of ice particles with some rock. They are held in an orbit around the planet by their own speed and by the force of Saturn's gravity.

Saturn is the sixth planet from the sun and the second largest planet in the solar system. It is made mostly of hydrogen and helium gases. It has at least 60 moons, including the most famous one, Titan. It is the only moon in the solar system with an atmosphere.

A Long Way to Go

Saturn is nearly twice as far from the sun as its neighbor, Jupiter. It takes almost 29 Earth years for Saturn to orbit the sun.

Saturn ⬇

Uranus, the seventh planet from the sun and third largest, was the first planet discovered by looking through a telescope. This cloud-covered planet looks like it is lying on its side. Some astronomers think a crash with a planet-sized object may have knocked Uranus sideways. The space probe *Voyager 2* visited the planet and helped discover many of its 27 known moons. It is believed that Uranus has 11 rings orbiting around it. These rings differ from the rings of Jupiter and Saturn. They are made up of large boulders of ice and small dust particles.

Uranus ➡

Did You Know?

Although Saturn's rings are more than 155,000 miles (250,000 km) in diameter, they are less than 0.62 miles (1 km) thick. If all the particles that make up Saturn's rings were pressed into a ball, it would be less than 62 miles (100 km) across.

In 1846, scientists searched for a planet they thought might be moving Uranus with its gravity. They charted where they thought this new planet might be. When they pointed their telescopes at that point, they saw a deep blue-colored planet with six rings and at least 13 moons.

Because of its blue color, the planet was named after Neptune, the mythological Roman god of the sea. Neptune is the last of the four giant planets and the eighth from the sun. The weather there is fierce, with winds that whip up to more than 1,250 miles (2,000 km) per hour.

▼ Neptune

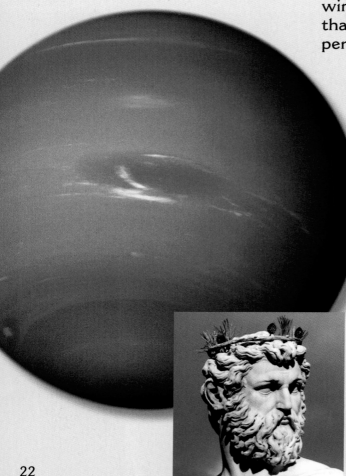

Scientists continued searching for more planets. They used the same methods that helped them find Neptune. In 1930, they charted where they thought another planet might be, and they discovered Pluto. It is more than 3.7 billion miles (5.9 billion km) from the sun. It takes Pluto 248 years to orbit the sun just once.

◄ Neptune, the mythological Roman god of the sea

Pluto was called Planet X until an 11-year-old girl in England suggested the name Pluto, the name of the mythological Roman god of the underworld. Pluto is tiny, just two-thirds the size of Earth's moon. Scientists argued about whether it was big enough to be called a planet.

For 76 years, Pluto was considered a planet. But in 2006, it was reclassified as a dwarf planet, a heavenly body that orbits the sun but has not cleared its neighborhood of objects in its orbit.

Did You Know?

Uranus, Neptune, and Pluto were not discovered until the invention of the telescope in the early 1600s.

Hello Pluto!

Spacecraft have traveled to the moon, the sun, and all the planets except Pluto. An unmanned spacecraft is expected to reach the distant dwarf planet in 2015. The mission is called *New Horizons*.

Pluto ➡

Night and Day

Pluto is so far from the sun that there is almost no difference there between night and day.

Dwarf Planets

After scientists found Pluto, they began finding more and more objects in the sky. They discovered countless planetlike bodies orbiting the sun. Most of these objects were found in the Kuiper Belt, a disk-shaped cloud of icy chunks beyond Neptune.

With all these newly discovered celestial bodies, scientists had to decide which ones were planets. First they settled on a definition of a planet: It had to be round, it had to orbit the sun, and it had to be the only object in its orbit. Celestial bodies that looked like planets but didn't fit this description were called dwarf planets.

Using this definition, scientists reclassified Pluto as a dwarf planet because its orbit crosses Neptune's orbit and passes through the Kuiper Belt. All sorts of objects are in its way. Pluto wasn't alone in its classification. Ceres and Eris (or UB313) were also labeled dwarf planets. Currently there are only three dwarf planets. But more may be discovered as scientists explore the entire Kuiper Belt.

Van Biesbroeck, also known as vB8B, is a brown dwarf—a star with so little mass that it will never become hot enough to ignite.

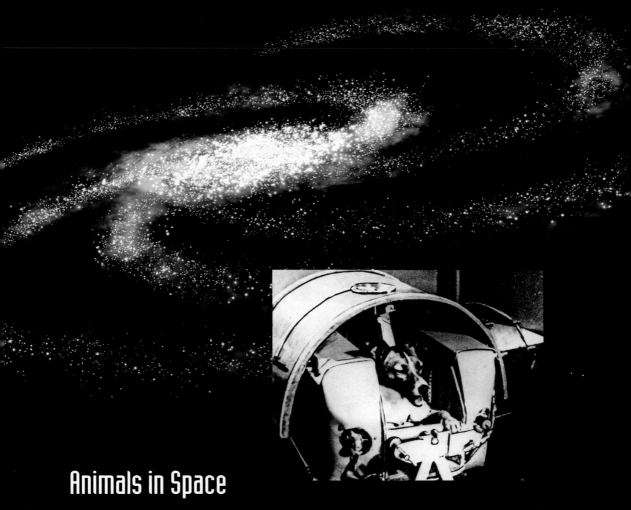

Animals in Space

It would have been more difficult for humans to travel in space if animals had not gone there first. Scientists studied carefully how animals reacted to conditions in space, which helped them prepare human astronauts. The first animal to orbit Earth was Laika, a mixed-breed dog sent by the Soviet Union in 1957. Her medical condition was watched from Earth, but she died in space.

In 1961, a chimpanzee named Ham was sent into space. He survived the trip, suffering only fatigue and dehydration. Because of this achievement, American Alan B. Shepard Jr. became the first successful American astronaut in May of that year. Without animals like Laika and Ham, space travel would have been far riskier for humans.

In orbit around the sun are many objects in many shapes and sizes. They were left over when the solar system was formed about 4.6 billion years ago. Sometimes their orbits cross the orbits of planets.

Asteroids

Asteroids are chunks of frozen gas and rock. Some are as tiny as pebbles, while others measure hundreds of miles in diameter. The largest asteroids look like small planets and are sometimes called planetoids. Smaller asteroids have more irregular shapes. Most asteroids are found in an asteroid belt between Mars and Jupiter.

Miss Mitchell's Comet

In the mid-1800s, most girls in America did not receive an education equal to that of boys. But Maria Mitchell (1818–1889) was different. Her father, a Quaker, believed strongly in equal education and provided Maria with many opportunities to learn. From an early age, Maria was interested in science and the stars. At the age of 12, she helped her father calculate the exact time of a total eclipse. When she was 17, she opened a school for girls and trained them in science and mathematics.

On October 1, 1847, Mitchell sighted a comet through a small telescope in an observatory her father had built. She was the first American to sight and chart the orbit of a new comet, which came to be called "Miss Mitchell's Comet" (its modern name is C/1847 T1). Mitchell, the first female professional astronomer, immediately became famous around the world. She went on to discover sunspots, stars, more comets, and the moons of Saturn and Jupiter. The Mitchell crater on the moon is named after her.

Meteroids, Meteors, and Meteorites

Meteoroids are hunks of rock and debris that orbit the sun at a variety of speeds. Sometimes they hurtle into Earth's atmosphere, trailing a bright tail behind. These "shooting stars" or "falling stars," as they are commonly called, are meteors. Usually meteors burn up while speeding through Earth's atmosphere. Some meteoroids make it all the way to Earth's surface, forming craters where they hit. Meteoroids that hit Earth are called meteorites.

Comets

A comet looks a lot like a glowing, dirty snowball. This mixture of frozen gases, dust, and ice dashes through space in a regular orbit around the sun. Comets, which are visible to the naked eye, create one of the most spectacular sights in the heavens.

When a comet nears the sun, some of its ice melts, creating a cloudy glimmer around it. The bright tail of ice, dust, and gas left behind can span millions of miles. The best-known comets are Halley's comet and Hale-Bopp, one of the brightest comets in our solar system.

An image of the Hale-Bopp comet was taken on March 7, 1997. It is one of the brightest comets of all time.

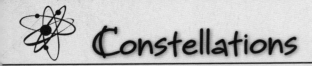

Constellations

Centuries ago, people used the positions of the stars to help guide them. For example, if people were facing the North Star (the bright star almost above the North Pole), they knew they were facing north.

They also found a way to keep track of the thousands of stars that were visible in the night sky. They mentally grouped some stars together and then connected them in a sort of dot-to-dot drawing. Each "drawing" was called a constellation. Constellations divided the sky into smaller pieces and made it easier to identify and locate stars.

Next time you look at the night sky, don't just wonder what's out there. Find some of the 88 constellations that light up outer space. Look up stories of ancient history and mythology. The variety of creatures, objects, and mythological gods drawn from the stars is fascinating.

If you look at the sky just right and connect certain stars, you might see a bear (Ursa Major), a scorpion (Scorpius), a fish (Pisces), or a compass (Pyxis). Or you might see scales (Libra), an eagle (Aquila), a lion (Leo), or a mighty hunter (Orion). Try pointing

How High?

When you release a helium balloon outside, how high do you think it will go? For a while, you can watch it rise higher and higher into the air. But eventually you will lose sight of it. Do helium balloons keep going until they reach outer space?

A helium balloon can fly very high, but it cannot go into space. As the balloon floats upward, the air around it gets thinner and colder. These changes cause the balloon to get larger. Eventually the balloon will burst, and the helium will escape into Earth's atmosphere. How high the balloon goes depends on how much helium it holds. Regular birthday balloons can rise as high as a small airplane flies.

out certain stars by their position in the constellation. Can you find the three bright stars of Orion's belt?

As you hunt for the constellations, maybe you'll spot Mars or a comet that no one else has ever seen!

The constellation Orion is one of the largest and most well-known star systems. From the northern hemisphere, it can be seen in the southwestern sky.

Stars and Supergiants

On a clear night, away from city lights, you can see between 1,500 and 3,000 stars. The largest stars are called supergiants—some of these stars are almost as large as our entire solar system. When these stars die, they blow up as a supernova and become black holes.

A star's color depends on how hot its surface temperature is. Red stars are the coolest, burning around 5,000 F (2,700 C). Our sun, a yellow-white star, burns around 10,000 F (5,500 C). The hottest stars are blue and burn as hot as 200,000 F (110,000 C).

While viewing the constellation Orion, the red star Betelgeuse can be seen in the upper left corner. This star is 60,000 times brighter than our sun. Rigel, a blue star, can be seen in the lower right corner. It burns 40,000 times stronger than our sun.

Science Activity

Collecting Micrometeorites

Did you know that objects from outer space may be found in your own backyard? Tiny bits of rock and dust from space constantly drift into our atmosphere. They may float around in the air for a while until rainwater or wind carries them to the ground. These smallest of space rocks are called micrometeorites. The best time to collect them is after a meteor shower.

Materials

- 2 heat-resistant, shallow dishes
- distilled water (about 2 cups—enough to fill a dish)
- magnet
- sandwich bag or plastic wrap
- heat source for boiling water (optional)
- magnifying glass or microscope
- 2 microscope slides and covers
- mounting glue
- eyedropper
- sewing needle or large pin

Procedure

1   Place a dish outside to collect rainwater. If there is no rain, you can just leave the dish outside for a few days.

2   Cover a magnet with plastic wrap or a sandwich bag. Sweep the covered magnet through the water in the collecting dish, especially the bottom and sides. (Micrometeorites are rich in iron, so they will stick to the magnet.)

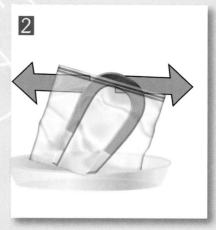

3   Fill a second dish with distilled water. Place the covered magnet in the dish filled with distilled water. Remove the plastic from the magnet and gently swirl it around to allow the micrometeorites to fall to the bottom of the dish. Remove the plastic from the distilled water.

4   Ask an adult for help and boil the water in the dish until it evaporates. You can also let it evaporate naturally.

5 Magnetize a needle or pin by rubbing it on the magnet for about a minute. Drag the pin or needle along the sides and bottom of the dish.

6 Tap the needle or pin onto a microscope slide so samples fall onto the slide.

7 Place a cover over the slide and glue it down. Examine the particles under the microscope. Any rounded and pitted metallic particles are probably micrometeorites.

Yuri Gagarin (1934–1968)
Soviet cosmonaut who was the first person to travel in space and the first to orbit Earth in 1961 aboard the *Vostok I*

John Glenn (1921–   )
The third American to fly in space and the first American to orbit Earth; after retiring from NASA, he became a U.S. senator; in 1978, he received the Congressional Space Medal of Honor; in 1998, at the age of 77, Glenn flew on the space shuttle *Discovery*, becoming the oldest person to fly in space

George Ellery Hale (1868–1938)
Founder of three great observatories: Yerkes Observatory in Wisconsin, Mount Wilson Observatory near Los Angeles, and the Hale Solar Laboratory in Pasadena, California; he helped build the first giant reflecting telescope that was installed at Mount Palomar Observatory and named the Hale Telescope in his honor

Edwin Hubble (1889–1953)
One of the greatest astronomers of all time, he discovered other galaxies in the universe and proved that the universe is still growing

Maria Mitchell (1818–1889)
Discoverer of the first telescopic comet (a comet too faint to be seen from Earth without the use of a telescope); also the first female astronomy professor

Lyman Spitzer Jr. (1914–1997)
First to propose placing telescopes in space; leading expert on interstellar matter, the gas and dust between stars

Valentina Tereshkova (1937–   )
Soviet cosmonaut who in 1963 became the first woman to fly in space aboard the *Vostok 6*

Glossary

asteroid—irregularly shaped body of rock that orbits the sun, usually in the asteroid belt, an area between Mars and Jupiter

astronomer—person who studies astronomy

astronomy—study of the universe and the objects in it, including galaxies, solar systems, stars, and planets

atmosphere—layer of gas that surrounds some moons and planets, especially Earth

comet—heavenly body that orbits the sun and leaves behind a bright tail of ice, dust, and frozen gases

constellation—formation of stars perceived as a design or mythological character

crater—bowl-shaped depression on the surface of a planet or moon caused by the impact of another body such as a meteoroid, asteroid, or comet

dwarf planet—spherical body in space that orbits the sun but has not cleared the neighborhood of objects in its orbit

Earth—third planet from the sun and the fourth smallest; the only known place in the universe where life is known to have existed or to exist

gravity—force that pulls objects with mass toward each other

inner planets—four planets—Mercury, Venus, Earth, Mars—whose orbits are nearest the sun

Jupiter—fifth planet from the sun and the largest in the solar system

Kuiper Belt—region of our solar system beyond Neptune, filled with small, icy objects that orbit the sun

Mars—fourth planet from the sun and second smallest; named the Red Planet because of its reddish appearance

mass—amount of matter in an object

matter—anything that occupies space and has mass

Mercury—planet closest to the sun and the smallest planet in the solar system

meteor—visible path of a meteoroid when it enters Earth's atmosphere, commonly called a shooting star or falling star

meteorite—piece of space rock that strikes a planet or moon

meteoroid—solid object floating in space

Milky Way—spiral galaxy in which our solar system is located

moon—natural satellite that orbits a planet; Earth's moon travels around the planet on an elliptical orbit and is visible because of the reflection of sunlight

mythological—based on traditional stories and lacking factual or historical basis

Neptune—eighth planet from the sun and the fourth largest

orbit—path of an object as it moves around another object in space

planet—solid, spherical mass in space that orbits a star such as the sun and has cleared its orbit of other objects

Pluto—dwarf planet whose orbit crosses Neptune's

rotation—one complete turn of an object on its axis

Saturn—sixth planet from the sun and the second largest

solar system—sun together with the planets, moons, and other celestial bodies that orbit it

star—luminous body in space made up of gases and held together by its own gravity

Uranus—seventh planet from the sun and the third largest

Venus—second planet from the sun and the third smallest

2296 B.C. Chinese record earliest comet sighting

1530 A.D. Nicolaus Copernicus writes *On the Revolutions of the Heavenly Spheres*

1577 Tycho Brahe views a comet, inspiring him to draw a cosmic model of the sky with Earth as the center of the universe

1605 Johannes Kepler formulates his Three Laws of Planetary Motion

1608 Dutchman Hans Lippershey applies for a patent for the first telescope

1610 Galileo Galilei uses a telescope to observe heavenly bodies and discovers four largest satellites of Jupiter

1786 Caroline Herschel is the first woman to discover a comet

1839 The Harvard College Observatory, the first official observatory in the United States, is built

1895 George Ellery Hale founds *The Astrophysical Journal*

1925 Astronomer Annie Jump Cannon receives the first honorary doctorate given to a woman by Oxford University in England

1929 Edwin Hubble formulates Hubble's Law, which helps astronomers determine the age and growth of the universe

1948	The Hale Telescope is opened on Mount Palomar, California
1957	Soviet Union launches *Sputnik 1*, the world's first artificial satellite, into space, beginning the Space Age
1958	Eager to join the Space Age, the United States forms the National Aeronautics and Space Administration (NASA)
1969	Americans Neil Armstrong and Buzz Aldrin are the first humans to land on the moon
1972	Astronomer Margaret Burbidge declines the Annie J. Cannon award because it is only awarded to women
1983	Sally Ride becomes the first American woman and the youngest American astronaut to enter outer space
1990	The Hubble Space Telescope is launched into space, 44 years after Lyman Spitzer Jr. first proposed the idea
2006	Astronomers decide there are only eight planets in our solar system and reclassify Pluto as a dwarf planet
2008	A powerful gamma ray burst becomes the most distant object ever seen with the naked eye; the explosion occured 7.5 billion years ago

Briggs, Carole S. *Women Space Pioneers*. Minneapolis: Lerner Publications Co., 2005.

Rau, Dana Meachen, and Nadia Higgins. *The International Space Station*. Minneapolis: Compass Point Books, 2005.

Rau, Dana Meachen. *Black Holes*. Minneapolis: Compass Point Books, 2005.

Somervill, Barbara A. *Nicolaus Copernicus: Father of Modern Astronomy*. Minneapolis: Compass Point Books, 2005.

Zannos, Susan. *Edwin Hubble and the Theory of the Expanding Universe*. Hockessin, Del.: Mitchell Lane Publishers, 2004.

On the Web

For more information on this topic, use FactHound.

1. Go to *www.facthound.com*
2. Choose your grade level.
3. Begin your search.

This book's ID number is 9780756540715

FactHound will find the best sites for you.

Index

Aldrin, Buzz, 15
Apollo 11, 15
Armstrong, Neil, 15
asteroid, 26
astronomer, 7, 18, 26
atmosphere, 14, 20, 27

black hole, 9, 29

celestial bodies, 6, 8, 10, 23, 24
Collins, Michael, 15
comets, 26, 27, 29
constellations, 28, 29
Copernicus, Nicolas, 6
crater, 12, 26, 27

dwarf planet, 23, 24

Earth, 6, 7, 10, 11, 12, 13, 14, 15,
    16, 17, 18, 23, 25, 27, 28
eclipse, 26
equinox, 16

galaxy, 7, 8, 9
gravity, 8, 9, 11, 20, 22
Greeks, 6, 8

hemisphere, 16, 17

Jupiter, 10, 11, 18, 26

Kuiper Belt, 24

Mars, 10, 12, 18, 26, 29
Mercury, 10, 11, 12
meteor, 27

meteorite, 27
meteoroid, 27
Milky Way, 7, 8
Mitchell, Maria, 26
moons, 10, 15, 18, 20, 21, 22,
    23, 26

Neptune, 10, 11, 22, 24
New Horizons, 23

orbit, 6, 8, 11, 13, 14, 17, 20, 24,
    26, 27
outer space, 6, 14, 28

planet, 8, 10, 11, 12, 13, 14, 17, 18,
    20, 21, 22, 23, 24, 26
Pluto, 22, 23, 24

rings, 18, 20, 21, 22
Roman, 8, 13, 17, 18, 22, 23
rotation, 10, 14

Saturn, 10, 20, 26
solar system, 6, 7, 8, 10, 12, 13, 14,
    17, 18, 20, 27, 29
solstice, 16
star, 7, 8, 9, 10, 28, 29
sun, 8, 10, 11, 12, 13, 14, 16, 17, 18,
    20, 21, 22, 23, 24, 26, 27, 29

telescope, 21, 22, 26
universe, 6
Uranus, 10, 21, 22

Venus, 10, 12,13, 14
Voyager 2, 21

Lisa E. Greathouse

Lisa Greathouse grew up in Brooklyn, New York, and graduated from the State University of New York at Albany with a bachelor's degree in English and journalism. She was a reporter, writer, and editor for the Associated Press for 10 years, where she covered news on everything from science and technology to business and politics. She has also been a magazine editor and a writer for education publications and a university Web site. She is married with two children and lives in Southern California.

Image Credits

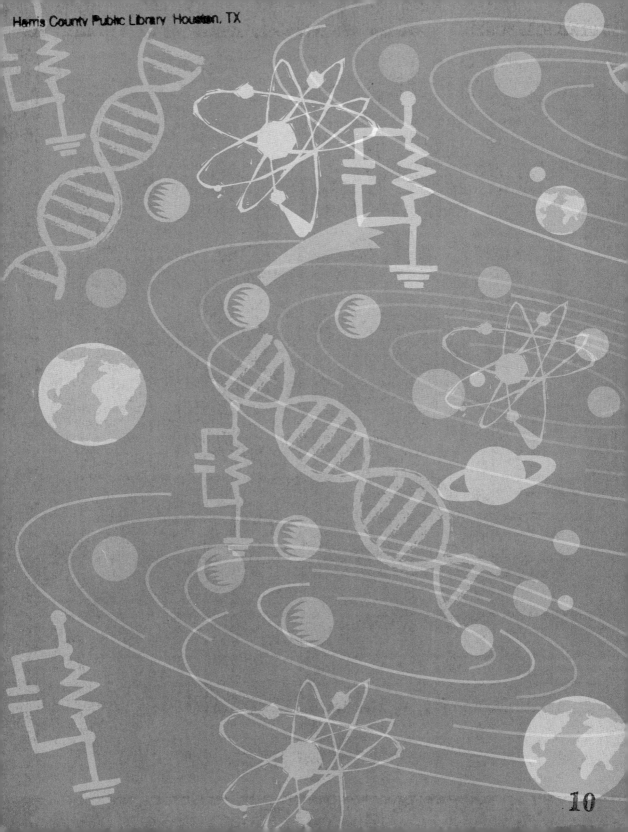